Awake, My Soul, and Sing!

A Service of Worship for the Easter and Lenten Season

ARRANGED BY JOHN PURIFOY
NARRATION BY MARY KAY BEALL

ALSO AVAILABLE:

Listening Cassette	DMC-7049
Preview Pak	DMC/BK-7049
Stereo/Split-Track Accompaniment Cassette	DMTR/S-7049
Chamber Orchestration	DMCO-7049
Full Orchestration	DMOR-7049
Conductor's Score	DMCS-7049
Handbell Packet	DMHB-7049

FULL ORCHESTRATION:
Handbells
Flute
Oboe
Trumpet 1,2
French Horn
Trombones 1,2
Percussion (2 timpani, sus. cym., orch. bells)
Violin 1,2
Viola
Cello
Bass
Piano, Organ (from vocal score)

CHAMBER ORCHESTRATION:
Handbells
Flute/Recorder
Oboe
Horn
Violin 1,2
Viola
Cello
Piano, Organ (from vocal score)

THE DESIGNER MUSIC GROUP

© Copyright MCMXCIV Brentwood Music Publishing, Inc., One Maryland Farms, Suite 200, Brentwood, TN, 37027
All Rights Reserved. Unauthorized Duplication Prohibited.

Cover design by Robert Mott & Associates

SEQUENCE

Awake, My Soul, and Sing!	3
Alleluia! Alleluia!	13
Holy Spirit, Truth Divine	22
Here at Thy Table	29
They Came to the Garden	38
O Love That Wilt Not Let Me Go	51
'Tis the Spring of Souls Today	59
Awake, My Soul, and Sing! (Reprise) *with* Crown Him With Many Crowns	68

HYMNS FOR CONGREGATION

Alleluia! Alleluia!	80
Crown Him With Many Crowns	81

Awake, My Soul, and Sing!

Words by
MATTHEW BRIDGES

Music by
JOHN PURIFOY
Arranged by
JOHN PURIFOY

© Copyright MCMXCIV New Spring Publishing (ASCAP), a division of Brentwood Music Publishing, Inc., One Maryland Farms,
Suite 200, Brentwood, TN 37027. All rights reserved. International copyright secured. Unauthorized duplication prohibited by law.
DISTRIBUTED BY BRENTWOOD MUSIC.

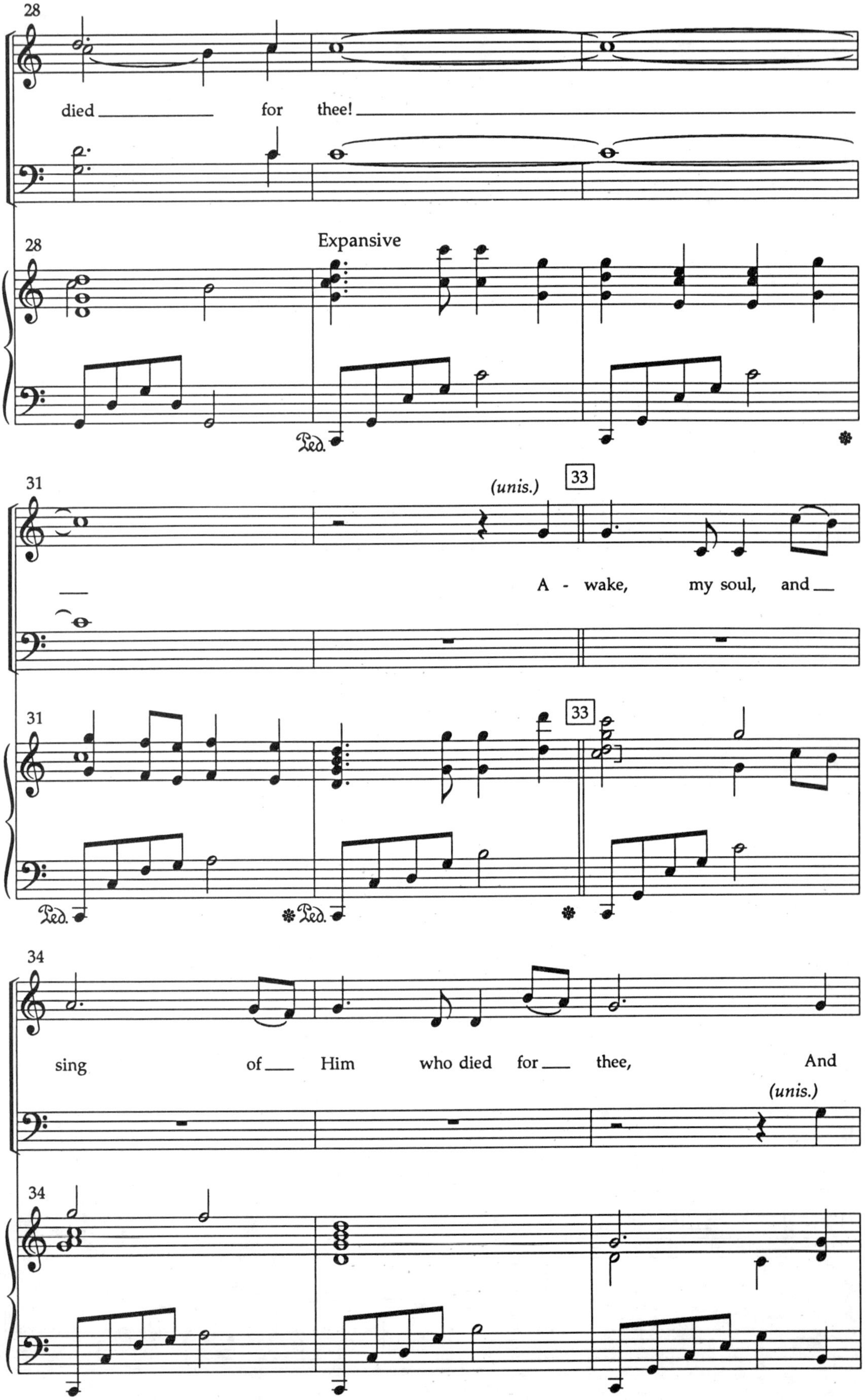

died ____ for thee! ____

Expansive

(unis.)

A - wake, my soul, and ____ sing of ____ Him who died for ____ thee, And

(unis.)

NARRATOR 1: Christ the Lord is risen today!

CHOIR: ALLELUIA!

NARRATOR 2: All creation joins to say ...

CHOIR: ALLELUIA!

NARRATOR 1: Raise your joys and triumphs high!

CHOIR: ALLELUIA!

NARRATOR 2: Sing, ye heavens, and earth reply ...

(Music begins.)

Alleluia! Alleluia!

Words by
CHRISTOPHER WORDSWORTH

Music by
LLOYD LARSON
Arranged by
JOHN PURIFOY and LLOYD LARSON

© Copyright MCMXCIV New Spring Publishing (ASCAP), a division of Brentwood Music Publishing, Inc., One Maryland Farms, Suite 200, Brentwood, TN 37027. All rights reserved. International copyright secured. Unauthorized duplication prohibited by law.
DISTRIBUTED BY BRENTWOOD MUSIC

14

NARRATOR 1:	When He came to Nazareth
	    where He had been brought up
	        He went to the synagogue on the Sabbath Day
	            as was His custom.

NARRATOR 2:	He stood up to read
	    and the scroll of the prophet Isaiah was given to Him.
	He unrolled the scroll
	    and found the place where it was written:

NARRATOR 1:	"The Spirit of the Lord is upon me
	    because He has anointed me
	        to bring good news to the poor.

NARRATOR 2:	He has sent me to proclaim release to the captives
NARRATOR 1:	... and recovery of sight to the blind
NARRATOR 2:	... to let the oppressed go free
NARRATOR 1:	... to proclaim the year of the Lord's favor." (Luke 4:16-19 NRSV)*
NARRATOR 1:	May this selfsame spirit ...
NARRATOR 2:	... the HOLY SPIRIT ...
NARRATOR 1:	... be upon US this Sabbath Day
NARRATOR 2:	... that Truth
NARRATOR 1:	... and Love
NARRATOR 2:	... and Power
NARRATOR 1:	... and Right
BOTH:	... may dwell within our hungry hearts.

NARRATOR 1:	When the hour came
	    He took His place at the table
	        and the apostles with Him.

NARRATOR 2:	While they were eating,
	    Jesus took a loaf of bread,
	        and, after blessing it, He broke it,
	            gave it to the disciples,
	        and said ...

NARRATOR 1:	"Take, eat; this is my body."

NARRATOR 2:	Then He took a cup,
	    and, after giving thanks,
	        He gave it to them, saying,

NARRATOR 1:	"Drink from it all of you
	    for this is my blood of the covenant
	        which is poured out for many
	            for the forgiveness of sins.

NARRATOR 2:	I tell you
	    I will never again drink of this fruit of the vine
	        until that day when I drink it new with you,
	        in my Father's kingdom."
	                  (Matt. 26:26-29 NRSV)*

* Used by permission.

Here, at Thy Table

Words by
REV. HORATIUS BONAR, 1855

Music by
RUTH E. SCHRAM
Arranged by
JOHN PURIFOY

© Copyright MCMXCIV New Spring Publishing (ASCAP), a division of Brentwood Music Publishing, Inc., One Maryland Farms, Suite 200, Brentwood, TN 37027. All rights reserved. International copyright secured. Unauthorized duplication prohibited by law.
DISTRIBUTED BY BRENTWOOD MUSIC.

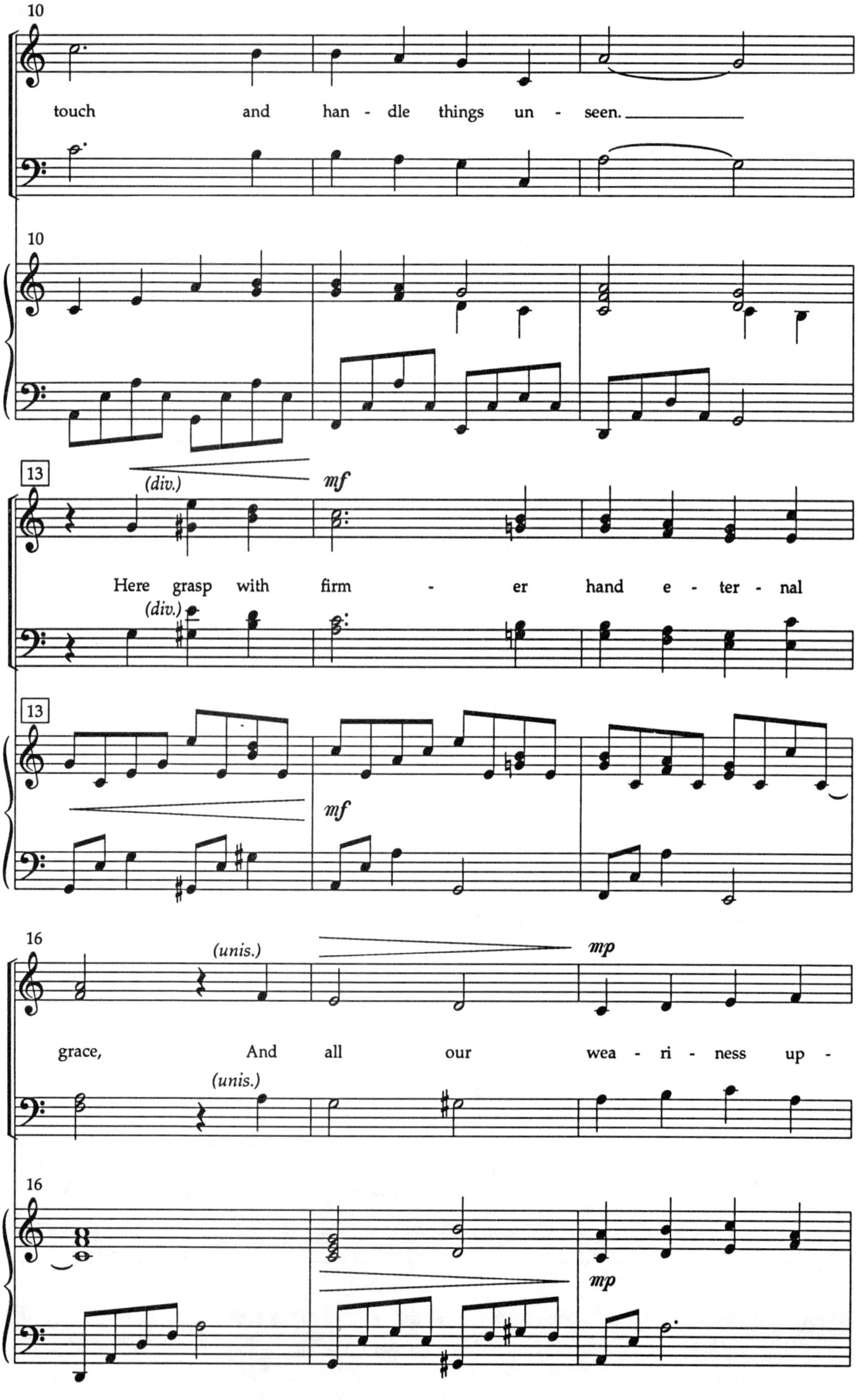
10
touch and han - dle things un - seen.
10
13
(div.)
mf
Here grasp with firm - er hand e - ter - nal
(div.)
13
mf
16
(unis.)
mp
grace, And all our wea - ri - ness up -
(unis.)
16
mp

NARRATOR 1:   After the Sabbath,
               as the first day of the week was dawning,
                 Mary Magdalene and the other Mary
                   went to see the tomb.

NARRATOR 2:   Suddenly there was a great earthquake;
               for an angel of the Lord,
                 descending from heaven,
                   came and rolled back the stone
                     and sat on it.

NARRATOR 1:   His appearance was like lightning,
               and his clothing white as snow.

NARRATOR 2:   For fear of him,
               the guards shook
                 and became like dead men ...

NARRATOR 1:   But the angel said to the women,
               "Do not be afraid;
                 I know you are looking for Jesus
                   who was crucified.

NARRATOR 2:   He is not here,
               for he has been raised as he said.
                 Come, see the place where he lay.

NARRATOR 1:   Go quickly and tell his disciples:
               'He has been raised from the dead!' "

NARRATOR 2:   So they left the tomb quickly
               with fear and GREAT JOY!

                                    (Matt. 28:1-7a, 8 NRSV)*

---

* Used by permission.

They Came to the Garden

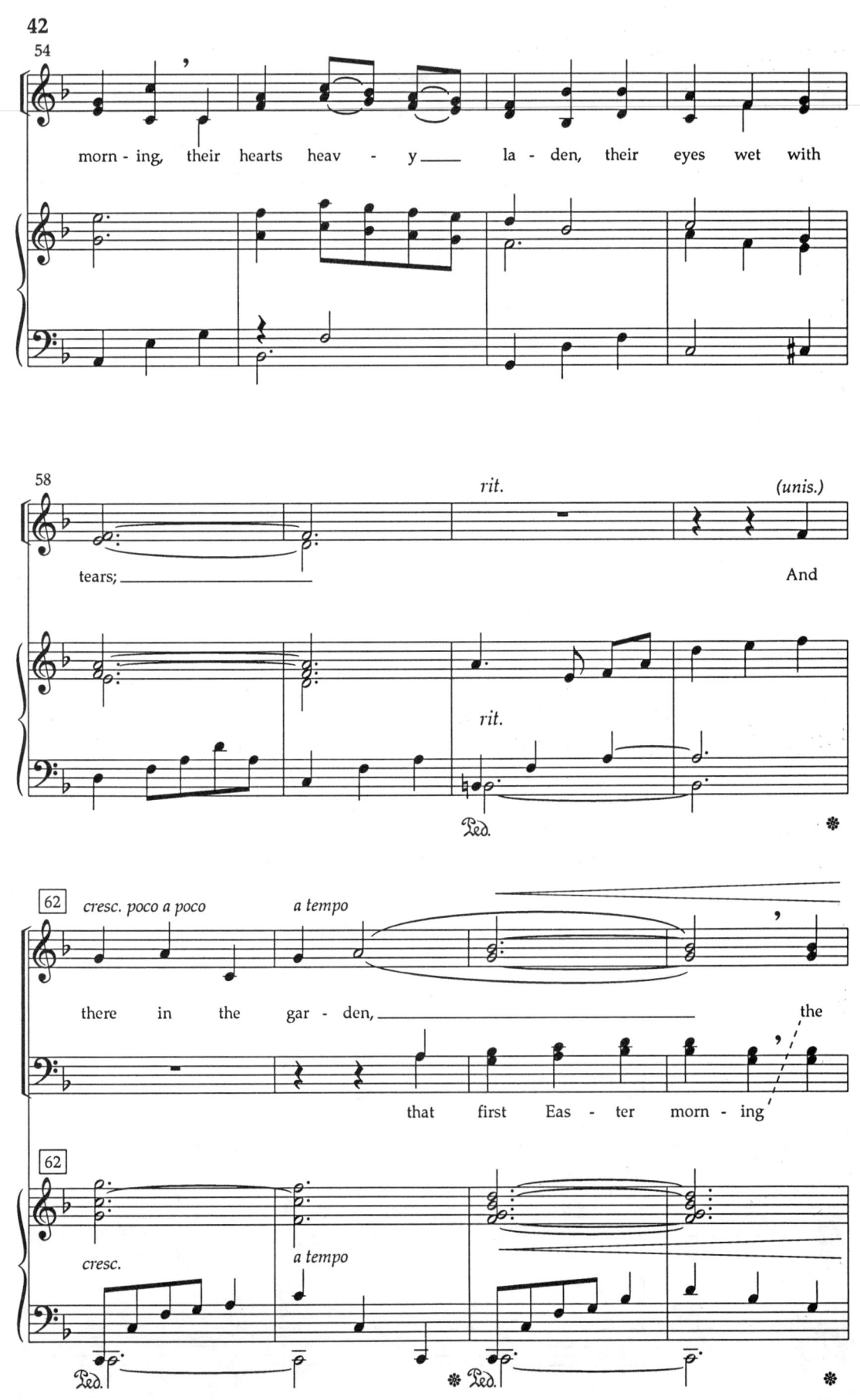

NARRATOR 1: How can I grasp Your love for me?

NARRATOR 2: ... a love that lights my pilgrim way

NARRATOR 1: ... a love that seeks my wayward heart

NARRATOR 2: ... and woos me when I go astray.

NARRATOR 1: How can I grasp such love as this?

NARRATOR 2: ... a love that pays the debt I owe

NARRATOR 1: ... a love that promises new life

NARRATOR 2: ... a love that will not let me go.

O Love That Wilt Not Let Me Go

(Soprano/Baritone Duet)

Words by
GEORGE MATHESON

Music by
ALBERT PEACE

Arranged by
JOHN PURIFOY

Arr. © Copyright MCMXCIV New Spring Publishing (ASCAP), a division of Brentwood Music Publishing, Inc.,
One Maryland Farms, Suite 200, Brentwood, TN 37027. All rights reserved. International copyright secured.
Unauthorized duplication prohibited by law. DISTRIBUTED BY BRENTWOOD MUSIC.

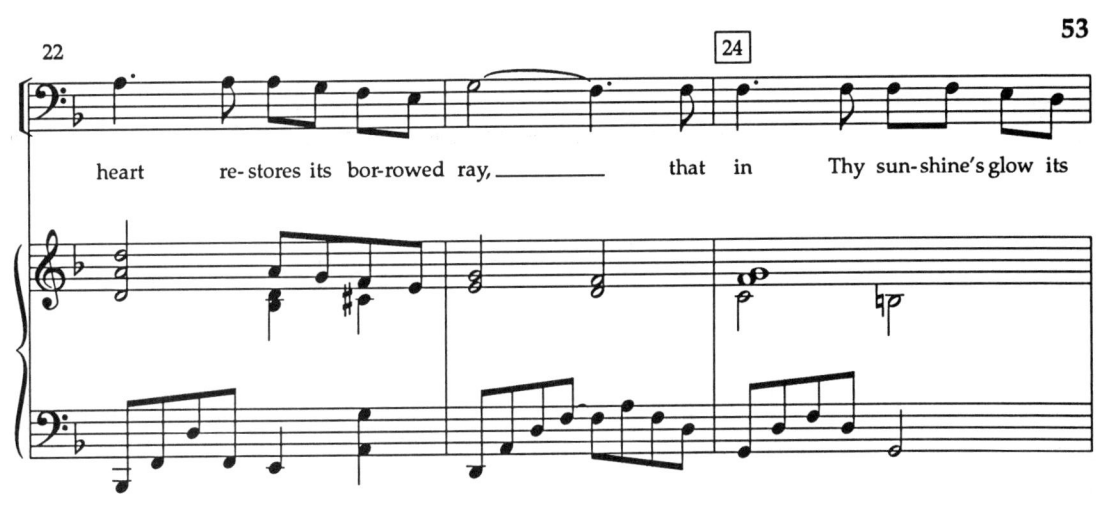

NARRATOR 1:   Listen! I will tell you a mystery.
              We will not all die, but we will all be changed ...

NARRATOR 2:   ... in a moment

NARRATOR 1:   ... in the twinkling of an eye

NARRATOR 2:   ... at the last trumpet.

NARRATOR 1:   For the trumpet will sound

NARRATOR 2:   ... and the dead will be raised imperishable

BOTH: ... and we will all be changed.

NARRATOR 1:   Then the saying that is written will be fulfilled:

NARRATOR 2:   "Death has been swallowed up in victory."

NARRATOR 1:   "Where, O death, is your victory?"

NARRATOR 2:   "Where, O death, is your sting?"
                                    (I Cor. 15:54b-55 NRSV)*

NARRATOR 1:   But thanks be to God

NARRATOR 2:   ... who gives us the victory

BOTH: ... through our Lord Jesus Christ.
                                         (I Cor. 15:57 NRSV)*

* Used by permission.

'Tis the Spring of Souls Today

59

Words from
JOHN OF DAMASCUS
(Trans. NEALE)

Music by
RUTH E. SCHRAM
Arranged by
JOHN PURIFOY

© Copyright MCMXCIV New Spring Publishing (ASCAP), a division of Brentwood Music Publishing, Inc., One Maryland Farms,
Suite 200, Brentwood, TN 37027. All rights reserved. International copyright secured. Unauthorized duplication prohibited by law.
DISTRIBUTED BY BRENTWOOD MUSIC.

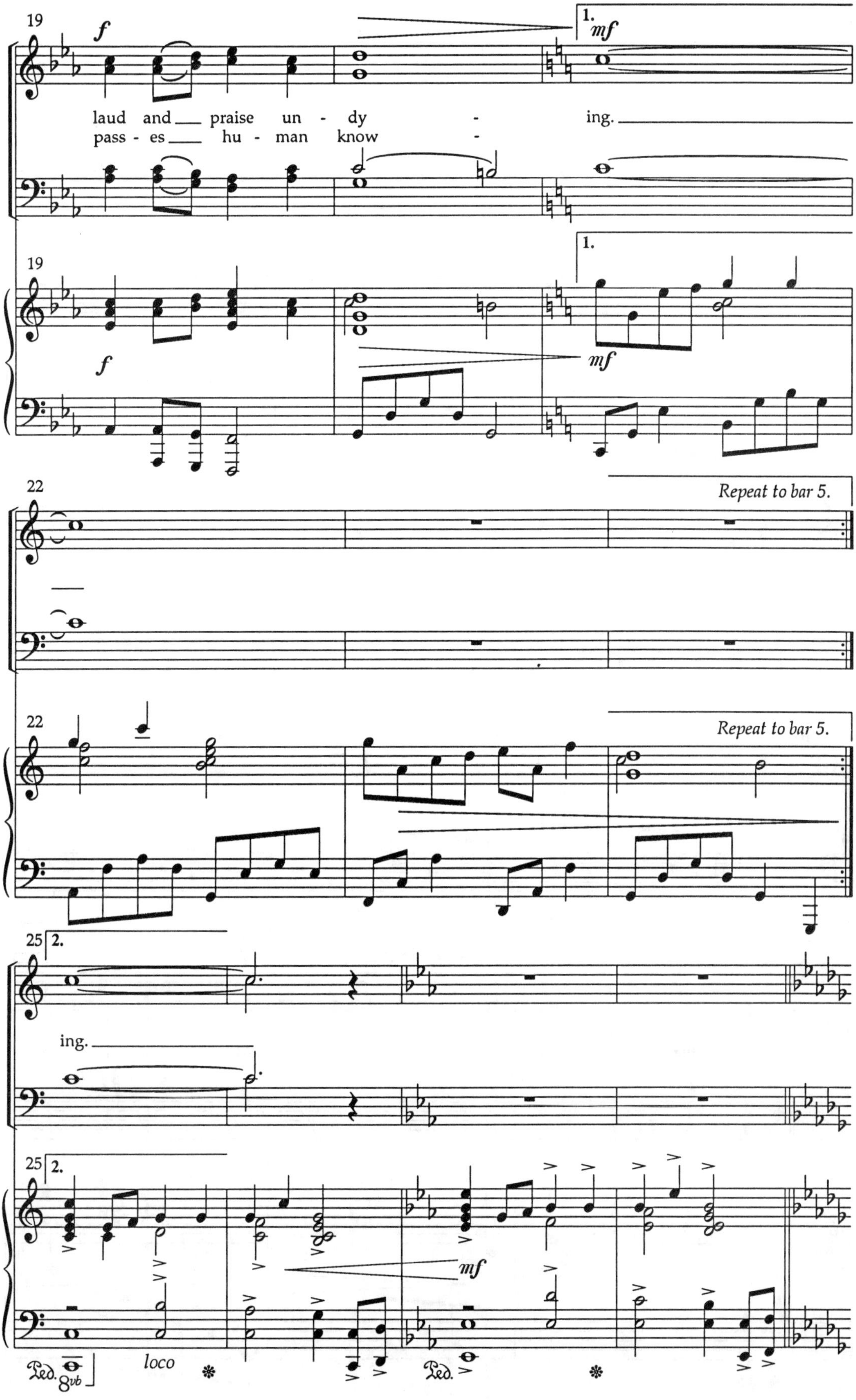
19
f
1.
mf
laud and praise un - dy - ing.
pass - es hu - man know -
22
Repeat to bar 5.
25
2.
ing.
loco

NARRATOR 1: Love's redeeming work is done! *

CHOIR: ALLELUIA!

NARRATOR 2: Fought the fight, the battle won!

CHOIR: ALLELUIA!

NARRATOR 1: Made like Him, like Him we rise!

CHOIR: ALLELUIA!

NARRATOR 2: Ours the cross, the grave, the skies!

(Music begins.)

---

* Text: CHARLES WESLEY

(Publisher grants permission to photocopy pp. 80 and 81 for congregational use.)

Alleluia! Alleluia!
(Congregation)

Words by
CHRISTOPHER WORDSWORTH

Music by
LLOYD LARSON

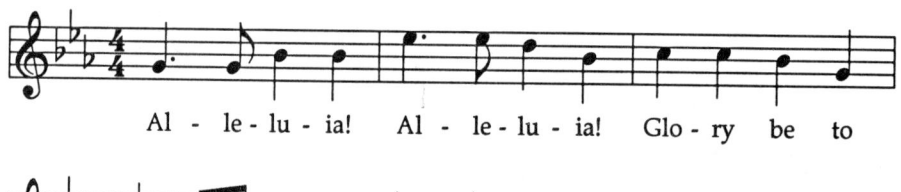
Al - le - lu - ia! Al - le - lu - ia! Glo - ry be to

God on__ high. Al - le - lu - ia to the Sav - ior

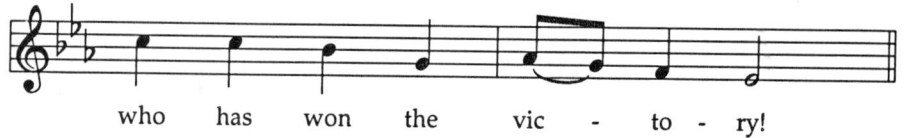
who has won the vic - to - ry!

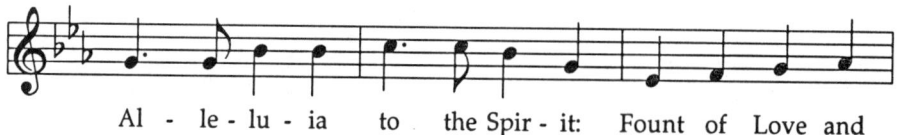
Al - le - lu - ia to the Spir - it: Fount of Love and

Sanc - ti - ty! Al - le - lu - ia! Al - le - lu - ia

to the Tri - une Maj - es - ty.

Arr. © Copyright MCMXCIV New Spring Publishing (ASCAP), a division of
Brentwood Music, Inc. One Maryland Farms, Suite 200, Brentwood, TN 37027.
All rights reserved. International copyright secured. Unauthorized duplication prohibited by law.
DISTRIBUTED BY BRENTWOOD MUSIC